Headlines

JOAN O'CALLAGHAN

Dedication:

In loving memory of J. Patrick O'Callaghan; journalist, newspaper publisher, husband, mentor, best friend.

HOUGHTON MIFFLIN HARCOURT

www.SteckVaughn.com
800-289-4490

10801 N. Mopac Expressway
Building # 3
Austin, TX 78759
1.800.531.5015

Steck-Vaughn is a trademark of HMH Supplemental Publishers Inc.
registered in the United States of America and/or other jurisdictions.
All inquiries should be mailed to HMH Supplemental Publishers Inc.,
P.O. Box 27010, Austin, TX 78755.

Rubicon
www.rubiconpublishing.com

Project Editors: Miriam Bardswich, Kim Koh
Editorial Assistant: Sarah Symonds
Art/Creative Director: Jennifer Drew
Assistant Art Director: Jen Harvey
Designer: Jeanette Debusschere

10 11 12 13 14   6 5 4 3 2

Headlines
ISBN 978-1-4190-2432-0

Printed in Singapore

CONTENTS

The New York [Times]

NEW YORK, TUESDAY, APRIL 16, 1912—TWENTY-FOUR PAGES.

ONE CENT

TITANIC SINKS FOUR HOURS AFTER HITTING ICEBERG
866 RESCUED BY CARPATHIA, PROBABLY 1250 PERISH
ISMAY SAFE, MRS. ASTOR MAYBE, NOTED NAMES MISSING

Col. Astor and Bride, Isidor Straus and Wife, and Maj. Butt Aboard.

"RULE OF SEA" FOLLOWED

Women and Children Put Over in Lifeboats and Are Supposed to be Safe on Carpathia.

PICKED UP AFTER 8 HOURS

Vincent Astor Calls at White Star Office for News of His Father and Leaves Weeping.

FRANKLIN HOPEFUL ALL DAY

Manager of the Line Insisted Titanic Was Unsinkable Even After She Had Gone Down.

HEAD OF THE LINE ABOARD

J. Bruce Ismay Making First Trip on Gigantic Ship That Was to Surpass All Others.

The Lost [...]

Chantal's got
Paralympic Games mu...
back to training, go sho[...]

The Scranton Tribune

WAR ENDS AS SAIGON SURRENDERS
U.S. Closes Out Costly Involvement

Helicopters Remove Last Americans From Saigon in Emergency Operation

35 Years Of Battle Is Ended

The Daily [Telegraph]

No. 30,548 LONDON, WEDNESDAY, JUNE 3, 1953 and Morning Post

Printed in LONDON and MANCHESTER

ELIZABETH II IS CROWNED
SPLENDOUR IN ABBEY SEEN BY MILLIONS
QUEEN 4 TIMES ON PALACE BALCONY: VAST CROWDS
ROYAL BROADCAST: PLEDGE TO SERVICE OF HER PEOPLES

THE SPLENDOUR AND SOLEMNITY OF AN HISTORIC WESTMINSTER ABBEY, WITH TRADITIONAL AND PAGEANTRY ALONG THE ROYAL [...]

The Globe and [Mail]

TORONTO, MONDAY, JUNE 26, 1950

Declares Reds Guilty

WAR IN KOREA

Fugitive Taken in Manhunt

U.S. Rushes Arms A[...]
Truman, Chiefs Confe[...]

By A. M. ROSENTHAL

New York Times Special to The Globe and Mail. Copyright

LAKE SUCCESS, June 25—The United Nations Security Council found North Korea guilty today of breaking the peace, demanded that the Communist government pull back its troops at once and called for an immediate cease-fire throughout Korea.

Ten members of the council—the Soviet Union stayed away—rushed to Lake Success for an emergency meeting and adopted [...] of the bluntest resolutions ever [...]

PARTLY CLOUDY. HIGH -7 C ★ MONDAY, DECEMBER 27 [...]

Insulin gives diabetes [...]

Feb. 11, 1922

TORONTO - Four doctors at the University of Toronto have discovered an internal secretion of the pancreas that is being heralded as a life-saver for victims of diabetes. They call the substance insulin. The research team consists of Dr. Frederick Banting, physiologist Charles H. Best, biochemist James Bertram Collip, and Dr. J.J.R. Macleod, a physiologist who had been supervising the research. It was Banting, practising as a physician in [...] who came up with [...] 1920. He had [...] that [...] dea [...]

Dr. Frederick [...]

University of [...] discovered a [...] anti-diabetic pa[...] is non-toxic.

Insulin is a [...] creas produces [...] help burn sug[...]

Quake in southern Asia: Giant wall of w[...] high, travelling 800 km/h leaves more than [...]

Waves of death

Devastation from south Africa to East Africa
Tremor called most powerful in 40 years

Americans' tsunami relief donations pass $200 million
Charity says online pledges coming in at $100,000 an hour

EXTR[A]

4

What is NEWS?

warm up

Did you read the paper or listen to the news before you came to school today? What struck you as the most important news item? Find out if your friends agree.

CHECKPOINT

What is the point made by Charles Dana? Is his example of news a good one? Why?

Charles Anderson Dana in *The New York Sun* of 1882, defined news this way:

> **"When a dog bites a man, that is not news, but when a man bites a dog, that is news."**

News is simply information. Long before there were newspapers, news was spread by word of mouth. Carvings in ancient cave dwellings were another means of recording the events of the day.

Some people believe that the word NEWS stands for North, East, West, South, meaning that news is information gathered from all corners of the world.

Everything that happens is a potential source of news — the usual and the unusual, the comic and the tragic, the great and the small. A news story can be about any event. Reporters and editors must be able to decide what makes news and judge the importance of a news story.

Reporters on the Job

Reporters are the backbone of the newspaper. With notebook, tape recorder, pen in hand, and sometimes a camera, they go out to cover stories when sent by an editor. Assignments are usually on issues or topics of interest to the public at the international, national, or local level. Reporters may also be assigned to cover special events such as the visit of a famous movie star, or breaking stories, such as an airplane crash.

Reporters are expected to provide the background to their stories so that readers can understand the issues. They are expected to provide information that is accurate and free of bias. They do not express their own opinions in their stories.

All news articles have a catchy headline, a byline that shows the journalist's name, and a lead paragraph. Often referred to as the "lead," the opening paragraph summarizes the story and draws the reader in. It is brief and simple. The rest of the story elaborates on the lead.

> **CHECKPOINT**
> What are the qualities of a good reporter? Jot them down.

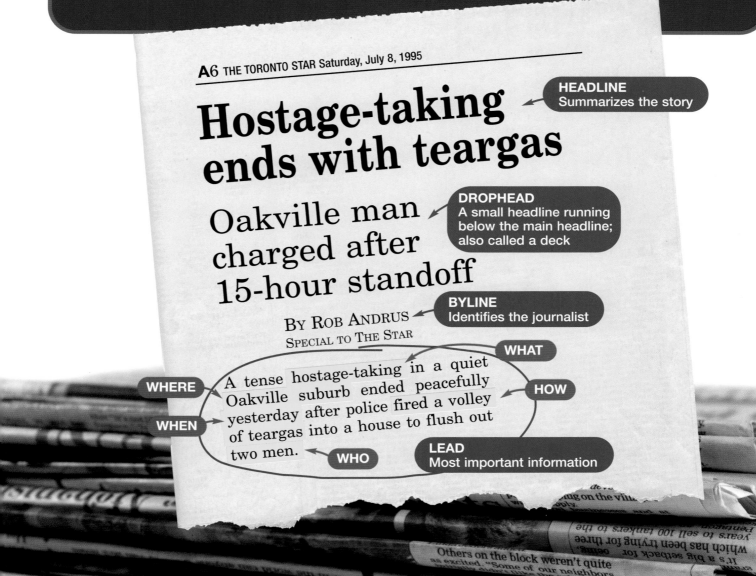

A6 THE TORONTO STAR Saturday, July 8, 1995

Hostage-taking ends with teargas

HEADLINE Summarizes the story

Oakville man charged after 15-hour standoff

DROPHEAD A small headline running below the main headline; also called a deck

BY ROB ANDRUS
SPECIAL TO THE STAR

BYLINE Identifies the journalist

WHAT

A tense hostage-taking in a quiet Oakville suburb ended peacefully yesterday after police fired a volley of teargas into a house to flush out two men.

WHERE
WHEN
HOW
WHO
LEAD Most important information

7

How the Newspaper Gets Its News

News can come from a variety of sources. A "hot tip" may be phoned in by a reader. Sometimes the newspaper editor may find under the door of his office a brown envelope containing a leaked document from a source that wishes to remain anonymous. Most of the local news gatherings are done by the newspaper's own reporters. Stories from other places arrive via the wire services to which the newspaper subscribes.

Wire Services

CHECKPOINT
Note the changes brought about by wire services.

In the early days of newspapers, correspondents — people employed to write material for publication — had to travel by horse, donkey, camel, sled, steamer, or train. A delay of two weeks or more, from the assignment to the publication of a story in the newspaper, was not uncommon.

Changes came about with the invention of the telegraph to dispatch news stories from distant places. The first news agency, Associated Press, was founded in 1848. During the Franco-Prussian War, an English newspaper sent dispatches by balloon. In 1870, Carl Reuter chose carrier pigeons to carry reports on the Siege of Paris. Reuter later founded another great wire service, Reuters. Today, wire services collect news reports from all over the world and distribute them electronically to newsrooms.

The Front Page and News Columns

Since thousands of news stories arrive daily in the newsrooms from a variety of sources, the newspaper's editors have a lot of important decisions to make. Editors must decide first of all what is going to appear in the newspaper. Then they must determine whether it is important enough to appear on the front page, or elsewhere in the news columns, and how much space to give each item.

To help make these decisions, editors run through this checklist:

wrap up

1. Using the information here, create a storyboard to show what takes place in the newsroom on a typical day. Use no more than five frames.

2. Read a short newspaper article. Then write a half-page report to address these questions: What happened? Where? When? To whom? Why? Also comment on the style of writing.

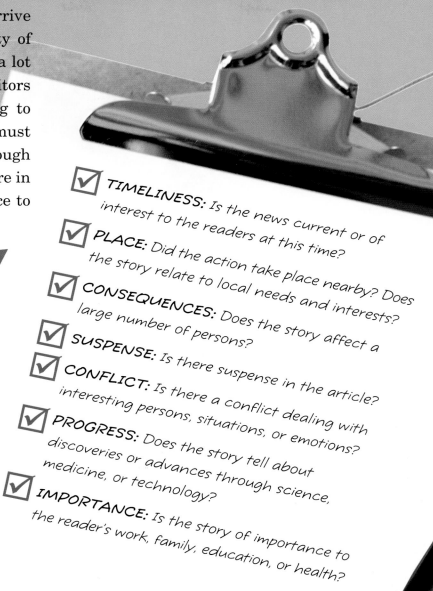

☑ **TIMELINESS:** Is the news current or of interest to the readers at this time?

☑ **PLACE:** Did the action take place nearby? Does the story relate to local needs and interests?

☑ **CONSEQUENCES:** Does the story affect a large number of persons?

☑ **SUSPENSE:** Is there suspense in the article?

☑ **CONFLICT:** Is there a conflict dealing with interesting persons, situations, or emotions?

☑ **PROGRESS:** Does the story tell about discoveries or advances through science, medicine, or technology?

☑ **IMPORTANCE:** Is the story of importance to the reader's work, family, education, or health?

Calvin and Hobbes

Monster's voyage of destruction

Devastation from South Asia to East Africa
Tremor called most powerful in 40 years
Many victims never stood a chance

NICOLAAS VAN RIJN, *THE TORONTO STAR*, DECEMBER 27, 2004

warm up

This article was written the day after the tsunami. With the class, brainstorm what you know about the effects of a tsunami.

A giant tsunami, rising silently from the deeps like a mythical sea monster, swept across southern Asia yesterday to turn a sunny Sunday morning into a scene of death and destruction across thousands of miles and nine nations.

The tsunami — Japanese for harbor wave — was triggered by a devastating earthquake, the world's fourth most powerful since 1900, deep under the Indian Ocean off the west coast of Sumatra, in Indonesia.

The wall of water, traveling at 800 km/h (500 mph) and towering in some areas as high as a three-story house, swept hundreds of meters inland, carving a swath of devastation through Indonesia, Malaysia, Thailand, Burma, Sri Lanka, India, Bangladesh, Maldives, and Somalia.

An Indian fisherman heard the monster scream.

"I heard an eerie sound that I have never heard before," recalled the man, who gave his name as Chellappa, 55. "It was a high-pitched sound followed by a deafening roar.

"I told everyone to run for their life."

The quake, at 6:58 AM local time, was enough to set the entire planet vibrating. ...

The first word from Banda Aceh, city of about 400,000 near the epicenter of the quake where 3,000 were killed, was terror.

CHECKPOINT

Remember this article was written the day after the tsunami hit. The world would learn that the numbers killed were actually much higher.

"People are fleeing their houses in panic, and the talk is that the river is rising," said one official, who hasn't been heard from since.

The victims never stood a chance.

---

swath: *broad stretch*   epicenter: *the point at which an earthquake hits the Earth's surface*

Scene outside a Buddhist temple, near Takuapa, Thailand, where more than 1,000 bodies were gathered (December 30, 2004).

"These big earthquakes, when they occur in shallow water, basically slosh the ocean floor," said Bruce Presgrave, a United States Geological Survey geophysicist. "It's as if you're rocking water in the bathtub, and that wave can travel basically throughout the ocean."

A tsunami just a few inches or yards high from trough to crest can rear up to heights of 30 to 50 meters (33 to 55 yards) as it nears shore, landing with devastating force. Actually a series of waves, a tsunami slows as it approaches the shallows of coastlines, but its height increases with terrible effect.

In nearby Malaysia the effects were felt instantly. A health inspector lost his wife and four siblings, swallowed by the sea

geophysicist: *scientist who studies the Earth*

during a beach picnic. Preschoolers taking an afternoon dip in usually placid waters were washed away.

The tidal wave sped 6 000 kilometers (4,000 miles) west across the Indian Ocean to smash into the East African coast, still with enough power to kill nine in Somalia, smashing homes and capsizing boats.

"All the planet is vibrating" from the quake, Enzo Boschi, the head of Italy's National Geophysics Institute, told Italian state radio.

It was, he said, as if a million atomic bombs the size of those dropped on Japan in World War II had gone off, with a blast so powerful it disturbed the Earth's rotation.

CHECKPOINT
Imagine the sound of one bomb magnified a million times.

More than 12,600 were known dead last night, with tens of thousands more injured, many beyond immediate medical help. Rescue officials expect the death toll to mount by thousands.

The underwater earthquake, which the U.S. Geological Survey put at magnitude 9.0, is the strongest since the 1964 tremor that struck Alaska, which measured 9.2.

At least a half dozen powerful aftershocks, one of magnitude 7.3, rocked the area, but the real devastation was wrought by the waves.

In Amblangoda, Sri Lanka, some 1 600 kilometers (994 miles) west of the epicenter,

the first of the big waves swept up out of the sea with a promise of life, washing the shores with the dancing figures of stranded fish.

But as young boys scrambled to collect the bounty, a second, more powerful series of waves crashed ashore, sweeping them away and bringing death for thousands more.

Sri Lanka, an island nation off India's southern tip, was devastated. Officials reported a death toll of 4,500, and said one million Sri Lankans, five percent of the country's population, are affected in some way — some in the most basic manner. ...

Railway tracks were washed away, buildings demolished and vehicles tossed like plastic toys. ...

wrap up

1. Using the information in this article, write a short definition for a "tsunami."

2. List the words and phrases that are used in the article to describe how terrifying the tsunami was.

3. Interview three people in your school and ask them what they think was the worst part of the tsunami's destruction. Write a summary of their answers titled "What was most scary to me."

WEB CONNECTIONS

Use the Internet to find the latest information on this tsunami. Include: death toll; countries affected; money donated. Make a chart to report your findings to the class.

Mom held, dad hit, daughters charged

KELLY PEDRO, *LONDON FREE PRESS*,
NOVEMBER 30, 2004

warm up

Share with a partner a time when you had a conflict with your parents. What happened? How was it resolved?

A late-night gathering of London teens ended on a bizarre note when a mother was locked up in her house and her husband assaulted — after they told their daughters to send their friends home. The two girls — police withheld their ages to protect their identities — became angry when their mother asked their friends to leave the family home near Highbury Avenue and Huron Street early Saturday, London police said yesterday.

When the girls' friends had left, their mother was locked in a second-story room, police said.

The father, who was in a different part of the house and unaware the mother had been confined, was punched, said Const. Jeff Arbing.

"It's very rare to hear about stuff like this," he said.

CHECKPOINT

The police constable described this event as "very rare." Why is this rare?

City police were called after the mother managed to free herself about an hour later, he said.

The teenagers were still in the house when police arrived, Arbing said.

No weapons were involved and the parents did not need medical attention.

Police have charged the teens with assault and forcible confinement. They cannot be identified under the Youth Criminal Justice Act.

forcible confinement: *locking someone up*

wrap up

1. Do you agree that the daughters should have been charged? Why or why not?

2. Working with a small group of your classmates, prepare and present a dramatization of the events described in the story.

Believe it o

Humans' ancestral tree

warm up

How would you react if you were told that your ancestors were like the hobbits in *The Lord of the Rings*? Compare your reaction now, and after reading this article.

ROBERT LEE HOTZ, *TIMES* STAFF, EXCERPT FROM *LOS ANGELES TIMES*, OCTOBER 28, 2004

On an isolated Indonesian island, scientists have discovered skeletons of a previously unknown human species — tiny, hobbit-sized figures who lived among dwarf elephants and giant lizards as recently as 12,000 years ago.

Experts in human origins called the discovery, made public Wednesday, of an extinct human species barely three feet tall the most important — and surprising — human find in the last 50 years.

"It is probably the most significant thing that has happened in my professional lifetime," said George Washington University paleoanthropologist Bernard Wood. "It comes out of nowhere."

paleoanthropologist: *scientist who studies human origins*

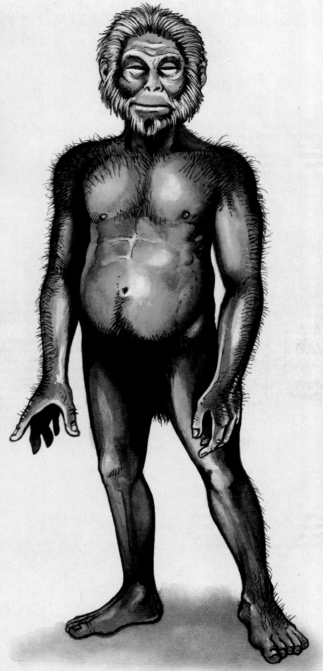

Artist's drawing of Homo floresiensis.

Illustration by Mike Rooth

r not
adds a twig

FYI

Java is an island in Indonesia, which is located in Southeast Asia.

Found last year in a deep cave on an island called Flores east of Java, the creatures had the smallest brains and shortest bodies of any known human relative of the last four million years. Yet, on the time scale of human beginnings, the skeletal remains were so new that the bones had yet to actually fossilize. The creatures lived at the same time as modern *Homo sapiens*. ...

of humankind commanded fire, cooked, chiseled primitive knives and axes, hunted in groups, and demonstrated other basic elements of human behavior despite their small brains, the researchers reported. ...

The first of the specimens to be found was an almost complete set of bones from a grown woman of the species, unearthed in September 2003. She measured 39 inches tall and had a brain measuring about 23 cubic inches, about the volume of a grapefruit. ...

The Flores specimens date from as long ago as 95,000 years to as recently as 13,000 years ago. The researchers speculated that the entire population was wiped out after a massive volcanic eruption 12,000 years ago blanketed the region with ash.

CHECKPOINT

Think of a phrase to replace "Homo sapiens" in the sentence. Then look up the definition. How close were you to the dictionary meaning?

The evidence of stone tools found near the remains suggests that this very tiny offshoot

fossilize: *turn into stone*

speculated: *guessed*

wrap up

1. With a partner, make a list of what was discovered in Flores, Java. What did you find most interesting and why?

2. Imagine you are a newspaper reporter and have an opportunity to interview Bernard Wood, the paleoanthropologist. Write down three questions that you would ask him, and explain why you chose these questions.

WEB CONNECTIONS

Your friend is visiting Java. Look up **"Tourism Java"** on the Internet and get information about its location, weather conditions, people and languages, currency, and popular tourist places. Tell your friend what you learned in a letter.

GIVING VOICE TO OUR OPINIONS

The Editorial Page

warm up

There are places in the newspaper where the editor and readers can comment and offer personal opinions. Where are these places in your local newspaper? Do these pages interest you and why?

The Editorial section expresses the opinion of the editor or the newspaper. It is printed under the masthead and the names of the editorial team. The editorial page is considered the newspaper's own territory. The main focus is the editorial and the editorial cartoon.

Editorials do not carry bylines. They are articles written by the newspaper's editorial team. They usually contain passionate or emotional opinions about public issues or topics and are written to be read, discussed, and debated.

A well-written editorial is really a well-written short essay. It has a thesis, a strong opening, a solid conclusion, and an orderly sequence of well-supported arguments to develop the thesis. It also has clarity of expression.

masthead: *the title of the newspaper*
thesis: *a point of view to be proven*

EDITORIALS HAVE DIFFERENT PURPOSES, AS SHOWN BELOW.

PRAISING: *It applauds an action, event, issue, or person.*

CONTROVERSIAL: *It opposes general opinion and is critical of an opinion, action, person, issue, or event.*

INTERPRETIVE: *It seeks to get at the underlying reasons and motives of an action, person, or event.*

EXPLANATORY: *It explains a difficult issue or event to its readers.*

HUMOROUS: *It seeks to entertain the reader by writing in a light or humorous way.*

INFORMATIVE: *It gives readers facts to help them make more sense of an event or issue.*

CALLING TO ACTION: *It calls the reader or some other person to take action, for example, to get out and vote.*

FYI

Early newspapers did not contain editorials. Editorial comment began as paragraphs following news stories around the time of the American Revolution.

The Editorial Cartoon

A standard feature for most newspapers is the editorial or political cartoon. The cartoonist comments on a political figure or a current event in a fun way. The cartoon provides humor, but sometimes it creates negative reactions from readers who disagree with the message or the sketch.

FYI

In 1867, the editorial cartoon first appeared as a regular newspaper feature in *The New York Evening Telegram.*

Frank and Ernest

Letters to the Editor

Dear Editor:

Unlike most other media, the newspaper offers readers a place to agree, argue, or present ideas and insights, in response to something that has appeared in the newspaper. This is the Letters to the Editor section. The letters appear on the Editorial page or very close to the editorials.

Most newspapers have policies that govern the selection of letters for publication. Editors often try for a balance of opinions on controversial subjects such as abortion, to avoid being perceived as biased.

perceived: *seen*

wrap up

1. Work with a partner to read an editorial or a letter to the editor in your local newspaper. Choose one that you find interesting, and share it with the class.

2. Compare the writing of an editorial with that of a news article. In a T-chart, list the similarities and differences.

WEB CONNECTIONS

Work in groups to research **"editorial cartoons"** on the Internet. Compile a book with at least five cartoons from each group. Include the cartoonist's name and the newspaper from which each cartoon is taken.

Parental Guidance

And until parents are fully on their side, school administrators around Alberta won't be jumping on the bandwagon.

> **CHECKPOINT**
> Can you guess what "jumping on the bandwagon" means in this sentence?

That doesn't mean the idea should just be abandoned. It just means that the results of a test project at Airdrie's Meadowbrook middle school are, as yet, inconclusive. …

Notably, more than three-quarters of the students surveyed thought they were doing better in school — even though their grades apparently didn't reflect that perception.

Perhaps what the students were trying to convey was increased enjoyment of their time at school — a factor that over time will almost certainly result in improved academic performances.

The same goes for teachers, who for obvious reasons are generally in favor of the change. And, as parents and students both know, happy teachers are better teachers.

Of greater concern — at least to parents elsewhere in Alberta, Canada — are the mixed reviews awarded the trial by Airdrie parents. A majority didn't like it.

warm up

By reading the headline and the lead, predict what the editorial will be about.

EXCERPT REPRINTED WITH THE PERMISSION OF *THE CALGARY HERALD,* MAY 31, 1995

A four-day school week will ultimately depend on parental support.

Kids like it. So do teachers. But parents — isn't that always the way? — aren't convinced that the future is a four-day school week.

inconclusive: *no decision has been made*
convey: *communicate*

Ultimately, parental consent will be the deciding factor in any school administration's attempt to move to a modified school week.

All of which means that any region in which the parents are split over the benefits of a reduced school week will find itself in turmoil if it tries to move to a four-day week without first building a consensus among parents — no matter what students, teachers, or administrators think.

modified: *changed*
turmoil: *disorder*
consensus: *agreement*

wrap up

1. What position does *The Calgary Herald* take? As a group, debate the pros and cons of a four-day school week.

2. Examine the editorial cartoon below. What is the message? Write a caption for the cartoon.

Editorial cartoons usually stand alone and do not necessarily deal with a topic elsewhere on the editorial page.

Letter of the Day

Train dogs, parents,

warm up

Why do you think people write letters to the editor? Have you done it yourself? In a group, share personal experiences.

THE TORONTO SUN,
OCTOBER 27, 2004

As one of the organizers of Saturday's demonstration at Queen's Park, I take exception to Michele Mandel's October 24ᵗʰ column ("The fur flies with pit bull owners") in which she criticizes a speaker for saying "Children need to be educated," suggesting the attitude of the owners is "blame the victim."

I believe that I have met and talked with many more pit bull owners than your average man or woman on the street. I have not yet met one who thought the victim of a dog bite was at fault.

CHECKPOINT

As you read, notice the arguments the writer uses to support his point of view.

Every single person I have ever talked to, without exception, has pointed their finger at one person only — the negligent dog owner who failed to contain, train, or socialize their dog, or all three.

It is important to remember that the majority (over 90%) of dog bites in this country occur in the family home, by the family pet, to the family child, or a visiting relative or neighbor. It is, therefore, not an unreasonable notion that a part of the effort to prevent dog bites would include teaching a child how to interact with a dog. We teach children not to hit and bite other children and we should teach them not to do the same with dogs.

Inside the family home, there are three parties that need to be trained: parent, child, and dog. The parent needs to realize that dogs and children are two different species, and that they should always be supervised. The dog needs to realize that it is at the bottom of the ladder in terms of pack position and putting its teeth on any human member of the family is not acceptable. The child needs to realize that there is a protocol that needs to be followed when dealing with a dog. If the

negligent: *careless*   protocol: *set of rules*

Pit bull–istockphoto

and kids

child is not old enough, then the responsibility falls to the parent to ensure safe interaction, and to the dog to be tolerant.

CHECKPOINT

Does this writer agree with the original article? How do you know?

It is an insult to every responsible dog owner (of pit bulls or not), and it is an insult that I take very personally, to insinuate that we have no compassion for the victim and that we, in any manner whatsoever, blame a child for the irresponsibility of a dog's owner.

Steve Barker
Dog Legislation Council of Canada

insinuate: *imply, suggest*

wrap up

1. Do you agree with the writer of the letter? Share your thoughts with a small group.

2. Write your own letter to comment on a letter to the editor, just like Steve Barker did. You could agree or disagree, and then express your own opinion. Read your work to a friend, and invite comments.

Arts & Entertainment

warm up

What would you expect to read about in the A&E section of the paper? What would interest you here?

C H E C K P O I N T

Does this sentence apply to you? What do you do to have fun?

HOLLYWOOD
PRODUCTION
DIRECTOR
CAMERA

The Arts and Entertainment section of the newspaper goes beyond reviews of books, movies, television shows, concerts, and plays. It is an exciting section, filled with information about the latest happenings on the entertainment scene.

Here you will find listings of events about dance, art, music, theater, film, and television. This is the place to read up about your favorite movie stars and pop icons, and the movies that are current hits. This is the section to get ideas on what to do for a fun night out.

The Arts and Entertainment section of newspapers have writers and reviewers who specialize in each art form. Their articles inform and entertain, but they also contain personal opinions that have an impact on the readers. A negative review of a concert or performance, for example, can hurt an artist, singer, or actor in ticket sales. And a positive review of a movie or book can dramatically increase its sales. As such, the reviewer must be aware of personal biases and not impose them on the readers.

In most papers, a fair amount of space is given to announcing and promoting local events. Newspaper editors understand that the interests of the community are important and must be taken into account.

All images—istockphoto

Movie Review

The Incredibles

S.J. SYMONDS, NOVEMBER 8, 2004

The Incredibles has the action, humor, and storyline of a real-life action movie. The only difference is that the characters are not real actors, they are modern cartoons. While the graphics are really great and kids will love them, the humor of the movie is more for teens and adults.

The Incredibles is a movie about a family of superheroes, living normal lives under the witness protection program. Mr. Incredible is getting restless in his job as an insurance agent and is eager for more adventure. And he does find adventure — the plot of the movie is propelled by the action and danger Mr. Incredible accidentally leads his family into.

witness protection program: *police program that keeps a person's identity a secret to keep them safe from danger*

The animation is so good; the characters look like three-dimensional plastic dolls moving around. And because they're not real, they can show off their superpowers with crazy chase scenes, amazing stunts, and unbelievable action.

The pace becomes slow in the middle of the movie, as we see the family in its daily life. But the ending is fantastic — very funny and full of great action. It's amazing to see these characters come together as a family and live out their destinies as superheroes.

wrap up

1. What does the writer like and not like about the movie? Would you see the movie? Why or why not?

2. Choose an article from the A&E section of a newspaper. Share it with a partner and decide whether you would attend the event or not.

AVRIL
— Growing up in the spotlight's glare

**Growing up is tough to do in the best of times.
Try doing it in a bubble with the entire world watching.**

warm up

If you had the opportunity to interview your favorite rock star, what questions would you ask? Share your questions with a partner.

MIKE BELL, *THE CALGARY SUN*, APRIL 1, 2004

For that reason, who couldn't forgive Avril Lavigne just a little bit for some of the petulance and attitude she dished out as she climbed to the top?

When the Napanee, Ontario native was doing her first round of interviews for her debut *Let Go*, she was uncommunicative, seemingly bored while offering one or two-word responses.

CHECKPOINT
What was Avril Lavigne like when she made her debut album?

Avril Lavigne–AP Photo/Rob Griffith

"Well, I was really young then," the 19-year-old Lavigne says during an exclusive

petulance: *bad temper*

interview with *The Sun* to promote her free show April 1 at Southcentre. "I was only 17 when I was just coming out. I've done a lot of growing up over the past couple of years. I'm not the same person I was."

Selling millions of albums worldwide, gracing the covers of international magazines, having your voice and vision broadcast continuously for two years on video and radio stations, earning awards, and even getting a place of your own — as she reveals she's just done — are the kinds of things that will do that to you.

And, at least during this particular interview, that maturity is on display. ...

But here, while the responses are only briefly longer, she at least seems engaged and not at all resentful of the attention, leading one to question if people were given the wrong idea of who she really is.

"I don't know," Lavigne says a little pointedly. "Do you think they did?"

While she doesn't have an opinion on how she was personally portrayed, the past couple of years there have been hints at how she was portrayed musically — more specifically how the production team of The Matrix and the singles they did ("Complicated," "Sk8er Boy") cast her as more pop, less rock. ...

"When we got them back that's what we got," she says, insisting once more for the record that she was responsible for most of the writing just not the production. "I kind of said to them before that I wanted to make it not so poppy, but there wasn't enough time." ...

"When I played them live I made them more rock. We were able to edge them up a lot ..." Presumably that won't be too much of a problem with her sophomore effort *Under My Skin*, due in stores May 25.

Lavigne describes it as "mature, deeper (with) piano-driven songs," one that was even written about her grandfather's death. Overall it's a much darker album. ...

"I'm really happy with the sound. ...

"I just did it all on my own. The label didn't come to me and say 'Oh, you need to work with these people' or 'Get started,' I just kind of did it on my own."

sophomore: *second*

wrap up

1. This article was based on an interview that *The Calgary Sun* reporter Mike Bell had with Avril Lavigne. Judging from the information in the article, write a list of questions that you think Mike might have asked Avril.

2. With a partner, interview each other about a special accomplishment in your life. Write your interview as a newspaper article.

WEB CONNECTIONS

Research Avril Lavigne, or another popular singer, on the Internet. Pick an interview with that person and in a small group, tell each other why you like the interview you chose.

Concert Review

RENÉE GRAHAM — MUSIC CRITIC
BOSTON GLOBE STAFF, MAY 25, 2005

Vintage U2 finds what it's looking for

Let's face it. In our increasingly troubled times we need rock stars more than ever. ...

Save for Mick Jagger, Bono is rock's last great frontman. He can be as delightfully cheesy as a Vegas lounge act or as sincere as a preacher, and he unabashedly enjoys every minute of it. Now comfortably in his 40s, he still has the raw energy of that mullet-wearing kid in the tight pants who first belted out "Sunday Bloody Sunday" in the early '80s. ...

Jogging along a walkway that surrounded the main stage, Bono's voice was a bit ragged at times, but he sang all out on every song, from "Beautiful Day" to "Bullet the Blue Sky" to "Sometimes You Can't Make It on Your Own," which he dedicated to his late father.

Naturally, he also spoke between songs, less chatter and more pronouncements

---

mullet: *haircut short at the front, long in the back*
pronouncements: *judgments*

about the state of the world. "We're very excited about the future, and we like to be in a city and state that has faith in the future."

He also dedicated "Running to Stand Still" to the "brave men and women of the United States military," and the song was accented with a rolling scroll of the UN's 1948 declaration of human rights.

Still, in an evening full of highlights, a standout moment came with the timeless ballad "One," during which thousands in the audience illuminated their cell phones; soon, the arena resembled the starriest of nights.

Several encores included "Mysterious Ways," "All Because of You," and "Yahweh."

For the early arrivals, Kings of Leon performed a hard, fast, loud set of songs from their latest album, "Aha Shake Heartbreak."

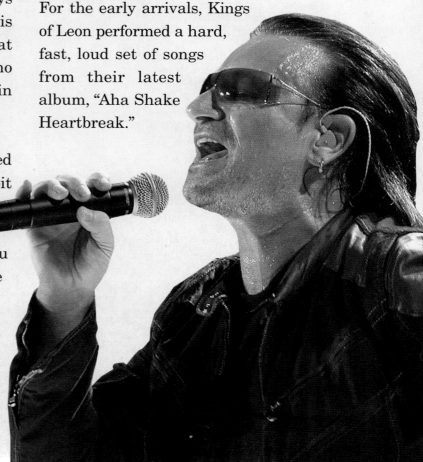

CD Reviews

BRIAN WONG — MUSIC CRITIC

CHECKPOINT

As you read, list the different elements that the reviewer comments on.

Kelly Clarkson: *Thankful*
(RCA, 2003)

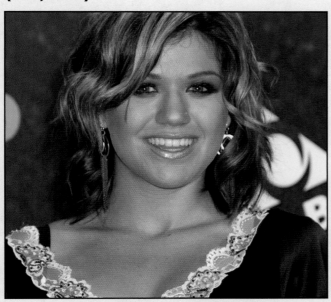

Winner of the first *American Idol* competition, Texas' Kelly Clarkson enlists the help of several songwriters and producers for her debut record, *Thankful*. As expected, the recording can't capture Clarkson's bubbly personality, but the album does showcase her gigantic voice. It isn't nearly as powerful as Christina Aguilera's — who co-wrote "Miss Independent," the cool, girl power anthem of *Thankful* — yet Clarkson's crooning remains warm. For the most part, *Thankful* aims for both stylized R&B and adult-friendly, country-tinged pop. The songs are safe and not particularly innovative, but they are an alternative to midriff-baring pop starlets, putting more emphasis on trained voices than trained dance moves.

crooning: *singing in a low, subdued voice*
innovative: *creative*

Kanye West: *The College Dropout*
(Roc-A-Fella Records, 2004)

After producing Jay-Z's album, Kanye West finally emerges with his own. *The College Dropout* is an exceptionally solid debut, mixing elements of '70s soul with West's laid-back rapping style. Guests on the album include Syleena Johnson, who lends her vocals to "All Falls Down," while Twista provides some speedy rhymes on "Slow Jamz," a song that pays tribute to smooth love songs. The disc climaxes with "Through the Wire," which West remarkably recorded while his jaw was still wired shut after a near-fatal automobile accident. Aside from some unnecessary skits between songs, *Dropout* is a stellar mix of old with new into a grade-A record.

CHECKPOINT

What are the things the reviewer likes about this CD? What does the reviewer not like?

wrap up

1. In a chart, show the similarities and differences between concert and CD reviews.

2. Choose any one of the reviews. Do you think the review was fair? Write a short paragraph to explain your answer.

WEB CONNECTIONS

Check out CD reviews for *Thankful* and *The College Dropout* on the Internet. Compare them to what you read here. Based on what you learn, write your own review of a CD that you own.

Book Review

Harry Potter and t

J. O'CALLAGHAN — STAFF REVIEWER, JULY 8, 2000

Harry Potter fans are sure to welcome this, the fourth in the series of Potter books written by J.K. Rowling. The familiar characters are back: Harry and his friends Ron Weasley and Hermione Granger, as well as Dumbledore, Snape, Hagrid, Draco Malfoy, and Hedwig, Harry's owl.

As usual, the book begins with Harry wishing summer vacation with his unbearable relatives, the Dursleys, would end quickly. The story then

Joanne K. Rowling at Harrods department store signing copies of *Harry Potter and the Goblet of Fire.*

he Goblet of Fire

moves to the International Quidditch Cup, where strange and frightening events occur.

At school, Harry learns that there will be no quidditch, his favorite sport, but instead, champions from three wizardry schools will compete throughout the year in the Triwizard Tournament. Questions arise. Who submitted Harry's name as a champion for Hogwarts when he was clearly underage? And why did the Goblet of Fire accept him?

Harry soon learns that his life is in danger from a ruthless and devilishly clever enemy. He will have to outsmart not only the champions against whom he must compete, but also the enemy who will stop at nothing.

Harry is growing up. In *Harry Potter and the Goblet of Fire*, we see for the first time, Harry, Ron, and Hermione experiencing the pains of first love. In addition many more unexpected things happen.

The reader will find this book as spellbinding as the earlier Harry Potter books.

Joanne K. Rowling–Photo by UPPA/ZUMA Press/KEYSTONE Canada. (©) Copyright 2000 by UPPA

FYI

Book reviews started in 1749 when Ralph Griffith's *The Monthly Review* urged contributors to not only describe books but evaluate them as well.

The Harry Potter books have sold over 250 million copies worldwide and have been translated into 55 languages including Latin and Ancient Greek.

At the height of Harry mania, *Harry Potter and the Order of the Phoenix* was flying out of stores at a rate of eight books per second.

J.K. Rowling is worth $1 billion.

wrap up

1. Choose a book you have read and write a review, using *Harry Potter and the Goblet of Fire* as a model. Invite a classmate to help you edit your review.

2. Collect all the reviews written by your classmates and put them together in a class binder. Refer to the reviews when you are looking for something to read.

WEB CONNECTIONS

Check out J.K. Rowling, the author of the Harry Potter books on the Internet. Create a profile of the author and her writing style.

THE NEWSPAPER'S PLAYPEN

warm up

Get together with a small group of your classmates and discuss the sports that you enjoy doing and the ones that you enjoy watching.

Sometimes referred to as the "playpen," the Sports section is one of the most widely read parts of the newspaper. This section provides information on many sports. These include popular sports — baseball, hockey, basketball, track and field events, tennis, swimming, horse racing, skiing, soccer, rugby, football, cycling, and boxing. Both amateur and professional sports receive coverage.

Covering sports for a newspaper is a challenge. With teams playing in major cities in North America and other continents, editors and writers run into logistical problems. An example is the time differences between the countries where games are played and where they are reported.

The quality of journalism on the sports pages has gone beyond the mere reporting of games that have taken place. The newspapers have their own sports reporters researching background information on games and players. They also include detailed statistics and an analysis of each game and club. For this reason, charts and graphs are an important feature of this section.

amateur: *non-professional, unpaid*
logistical: *organizational*

The sportswriter, like the TV or radio sports commentator, seeks to capture the excitement of a game for readers or listeners who are not there in person. Sportswriters are usually sports fans themselves and are familiar with every aspect of the game they specialize in.

Because of its spectacular nature, sports pages contain brilliant photographs that capture the actions of players, and the emotions of victories and defeats. Sports fans love their sports passionately; it doesn't matter if they don't actually play the game.

To add a touch of humor, the sports section carries sports cartoons that give an interesting perspective to a sport or a game. This is one feature that even non-sports fans can appreciate and have a good laugh at.

WEB CONNECTIONS

On the Internet, key in **"sportswriter"** and read about what it takes to be one. Do you have the qualities to be a sportswriter? Would you like to be one? Why or why not?

wrap up

1. Look through the sports pages for photographs. Choose at least three of them, and write a caption for each. Make a collection of all work done by the class and display it.

2. Working with a partner, pretend to be a famous sports personality and reporter. Write the interview questions and answers, and then do a role-play for the class. Be sure to speak and act like the real personalities.

Canadian juniors loaded with talent

NHL-caliber players included on big, skillful squad

Canada's World Junior Hockey teammates — left to right — Corey Perry, Patrice Bergeron, Sidney Crosby, and Dion Phaneuf.

Canadian Juniors–CP PHOTO/Jonathan Hayward

warm up

Check out the headlines. What skills would you expect from "NHL-caliber players"?

THE CANADIAN PRESS, *KITCHENER-WATERLOO RECORD*, DECEMBER 17, 2004

Best Canadian junior team ever? It should be.

With NHL-caliber players and more veterans in the lineup than any Canadian junior squad before, this team's challenge will be to try to turn all that potential into gold.

Brent Sutter, an 18-year NHL veteran and two-time Stanley Cup winner, is in charge of forging the players into a unit better than the sum of its parts and, with this group of players, that's saying something.

CHECKPOINT

As you read, notice the skills and qualities that this team has.

"We're big, we've got good skill and I think we have the right mix of character guys here on the hockey club," the coach of the Red Deer Rebels said yesterday after naming 23 players to his team.

Canada opens the 2005 world under-20 championship against Slovakia on Dec. 25.

This squad will play the tight-checking, uptempo game typical of Canadian teams.

That style has got Canada close to the top of the podium over the last six years with four silver and two bronze medals.

"We're going to be a high-energy team, we're going to be in your face, and we're going to be hitting everything that moves," said winger Corey Perry. "We're also a skilled hockey club. There's a lot of guys that can put numbers on the board and it's going to be unbelievable to watch." ...

"With the NHL lockout, there's a lot of guys here who would be in the NHL right now," said Boston Bruins forward Patrice Bergeron. ...

Talent, skill, speed, and experience, combined with the fact the tournament is close to home — eliminating jet lag — and will be played on the smaller North American ice surface at the University of North Dakota, make expectations high both within the team and outside it. ...

wrap up

Write an email to a friend convincing him/her to go with you to North Dakota to support the Canadian Juniors in the 2005 world championship.

WEB CONNECTIONS

Search the Internet to find out which teams were medal winners in the tournament. What were the deciding factors in the gold medal game?

CANADA'S JUNIORS

A quick look at the 2005 Canadian junior men's hockey team:

Average age — 19 years, five months, 28 days
Average height — Six foot one
Average weight — 205 pounds
League breakdown — WHL, 14; OHL, 6; QMJHL, 2; AHL, 1
Oldest, youngest — Jeff Carter, turns 20 on Jan. 1; Sidney Crosby, 17

Red Sox conquer the world

warm up

Popular sports championships (the World Series, Stanley Cup, Super Bowl) are usually featured on the front page of a newspaper. Why do you think such stories are placed outside the sports section?

Boston Red Sox players celebrate after beating the St. Louis Cardinals 3-0 in Game 4 to win the World Series.

J. O'CALLAGHAN, OCTOBER 28, 2004

Last night's win by the Boston Red Sox over the rival St. Louis Cardinals was the signal for people all over the state of Massachusetts to begin celebrating, an opportunity they have not had for 86 years. The 3-0 win in St. Louis clinched the World Series championship for the Sox and they did it cleanly — in a four-game sweep. The last time Boston won the World Series was in 1918.

CHECKPOINT
What was special about this win?

clinched: *sealed; secured victory*

Church bells rang in cities all over the state while car horns on the streets of Boston blared in triumph. In the Red Sox dressing room, champagne corks popped as players and staff alike toasted their historic win and one another. "This is like an alternate reality," said Sox owner John W. Henry, soaked in champagne. "All of our fans waited their entire lives for this."

It was a win that put the cap to a nail-biter season. The Sox pulled off the greatest comeback in baseball history by beating the favored — and hated — New York Yankees

Red Sox–AP Photo/Al Behrman

No Cardinal pitcher could last more than six innings against the mighty Red Sox.

The win ensured that Manny Ramirez, who hit .412 with a home-run and four RBIs (runs batted in) would be named World Series MVP (Most Valuable Player).

The largest celebration in Boston's 374-year history is expected to happen tomorrow when the team is honored with a parade and championship ceremony. Statues are already on order.

CHECKPOINT

Notice how the the victory is celebrated.

Next April 11, when the Sox play their 2005 season home opener, World Series rings will be presented to the team and the 2004 World Series championship flag will be raised over Fenway Park.

in four straight games to win the American League Championship and proceed to the World Series against the Cards.

The Sox went on to beat the Cards three times in the first three games of the World Series matchup. The odds were in their favor that they would win the championship. No team in hardball history has ever been able to win the World Series after losing all of the first three games.

The Sox didn't fall behind the Cardinals in one single inning of the four-game sweep.

wrap up

1. What have you learned from this article about: the World Series, the Red Sox, and the St. Louis Cardinals? List in point form.

2. Assume you were at the game when the Red Sox won the World Series. Write a letter to a friend in another country who knows nothing about baseball. Describe the game and why it was so exciting. You could add more information about this game by searching the Internet.

ADVERTISI

warm up

Think of the role that advertising plays in your life. What are the things you buy as a result of advertising?

FYI

The first newspaper advertisement appeared in 1868.

Did you know that newspapers do not make most of their profit from newspaper sales? Actually, between 60 and 80 percent of their revenue comes from advertising. No wonder advertisements are on almost every page.

DISPLAY ADVERTISING

Retail or display advertisements often take up a big space on a page. The purpose is to introduce or promote a product, and to attract buyers and increase sales. Display ads are often in color, and they cost advertisers a lot of money. The larger the newspaper's circulation, the more it charges for its advertising.

CLASSIFIED ADVERTISING

Most classified ads are sold by the number of words or lines. They are printed in smaller type, and usually without color. Classifieds are used by individuals or small business owners to announce jobs or to sell homes, cars, and household or personal items.

Personal announcements are a part of classified advertising. The purpose is to convey special messages to friends or associates — about engagements, graduations, anniversaries, births, or deaths. Classified ads are also used to announce community or social events.

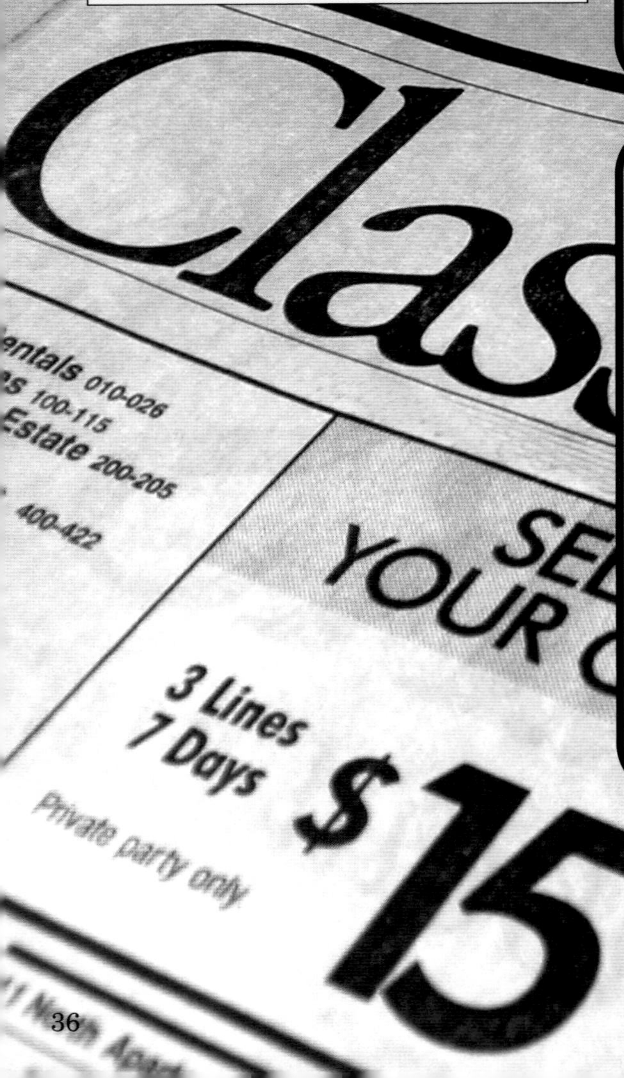

GOOD ADVERTISING DESIGN

☑ **DESIGN:** uncluttered and easy to look at — takes the reader's eye easily from the headline to the illustration, description, price, and store's name

☑ **DOMINANT ELEMENT:** a large headline, photo, or illustration that will grab a reader's attention

☑ **HEADLINE:** answers the consumer's first question: "What's in it for me?"

☑ **COPY:** effectively written message

☑ **LOGO:** allows the readers to identify the advertiser

☑ **LAYOUT:** effective use of fonts and white space

☑ **CALL TO ACTION:** gives the reader more information — sale, discount, bonus, coupon, map of location, etc.

wrap up

1. Study the two types of ads on the previous page. In a sentence, explain what each tells you about newspaper advertising.

2. With a partner, create a display ad of a product that you would love to have. Include an effective headline, the ad copy, an attractive layout, and a picture. Display your ad in the class.

Sample Ads

warm up

Think of some advertisements. What makes them memorable?

If you're close enough to read this, you've made the same mistake five-year-old Tina Phillips made before she was severely mauled.

Help prevent dog bites at www.humanesociety.com

PROTECTING CHILDREN AND DOGS

HUMANE SOCIETY of CANADA

FYI

This is a public service announcement. It is not selling a product, but it informs people about a helpful service. This kind of promotional message does not always cost money to advertise in the newspaper.

DEATHS

UNDER, Six Feet. Sadly, on June 3, 2002 Season Two of the Golden Globe winning series *Six Feet Under* passed peacefully under the beloved watch of friends and fans. Predeceased by Season One, Season Two was always spoken of with great admiration and will be mourned deeply. The season will be dearly remembered in rebroadcasts starting February 26th and is thankfully survived by a healthy new Third Season (premiering Tuesday, March 4th, at 9 pm ET on The Movie Network) that will live on in the spirit and loving memory of its predecessors. Donations can be made to your local satellite or cable provider. Telephone condolences can be directed to 1-800-565-MOVIES.

CHECKPOINT

Notice this ad is set up like a classified ad. Do you think it is effective?

What if kids pressured us the way we pressure them?

www.canadianhockey.ca

CANADIAN HOCKEY ASSOCIATION • RELAX, IT'S JUST A GAME • CANADA

Classified

BED single. Complete with mattress, frame, headboard and footboard. $150. 416-555-1234.

CDs! Lots of different tastes! $2 each. 416-555-6543.

DESK, white with six drawers and a matching chair. $50. 905-555-7890.

OLD STEREO parts, amplifiers, receivers, turntables, speakers. Up to $299. 416-555-2468.

TANNING bed for sale. 30 bulbs & two face lamps. 7 ft. long. Fan. 2 yrs. old. Must sell! $4000. Call 416-555-3547

XBOX. Complete with hand controls, and two games. $100. Call soon! 416-555-1357.

Obituary

LYONS, DANIEL — died peacefully at Capitol City General Hospital in his 89th year. Beloved husband of Hannah, dear father of Joseph and Marion Lyons, loving grandfather of Peter, Michael and Sarah Lyons. Mr. Lyons was a captain in the Royal Air Force, he flew 10 missions during World War II. He will be missed by his family and many friends. Funeral services will be held at Morton's Funeral Home on December 10 at 2 p.m. Instead of flowers, please donate to the charity of your choice.

wrap up

1. Which ad do you find the most effective? Write a list of reasons why.

2. Design your own ad for a product. Be sure to include all the elements that were on the list on page 37.

Lifestyle

warm up

What would you expect to read in the Lifestyle section of a newspaper? Do you think this section would appeal to both adults and teenagers and why?

There was a time when news and articles considered of interest to women were segregated from the rest of the newspaper. They were shoved away in so-called "Women's sections" that were dominated by stories about child care, cooking, and other "softer" features. Just as the Sports section was for men, the women had their own section for topics that were seen as exclusively feminine.

The rise of feminism led to the demise of Women's sections. Recipes and household hints, while still

demise: end

well just accept it all. There ... things we simply can't alter, ... how much we try. And the ... worry about it, the worse it gets. You're upset now, but once you get used to it, you will like it a lot.

AQUARIUS (Jan. 21 – Feb. 19)
It is not possible to know the future. Time can change a great deal between now and then. Great changes are happening and will continue to happen in your world. You may not understand it all but, if your instincts tell you to trust your future — then trust it.

PISCES (Feb. 20 – March 20)
The world would be a dull place without the unexpected, the unknown and impossible situations. A solution you are hankering after is so close. Much is now changing and, as it does, it will bring that elusive thing you desire.

...dent
...mat-
...a vi-
...sun,
...way
...ng.

...v. 22)
...eeds strong-willed
...raid to take on big
... You need to ensure the
... to an unfolding
... seems effectively
...nds. ...'t's deceptive. You
...stron... nfluence.

... Dec. 21)
...wh... ou are overstep-
... storing up trou-
...mark... you draw a line
...ture. S... lge in a good
...yourse... om Venus is a
...gic. Keep

★★★★★

important, were boosted by other features that truly reflected the lives and concerns of modern women. Women's pages became Lifestyle sections.

Gone are the days when recipes were the key to the page. The range of interests has expanded to reflect the interests and lifestyles of modern readers, both men and women.

The Ann Landers/Dear Abby type of advice columns, along with horoscopes, still have their place in the Lifestyle pages. Some newspapers still replace their Lifestyle section at least once a week with a Food or a Fashion section. Health issues receive a lot of attention, as do features on educational issues, child-rearing, and the teen years.

Lifestyle sections usually have regular columnists in addition to the advice columnists. Generally, a Lifestyle section has its own editor, responsible for assigning feature themes and for drawing together each day's material. In most newspapers, today's Lifestyle section makes good use of color photographs and illustrations and has the same professional touch of journalism as every other segment.

The Lifestyle section is one that strives to reflect and address changes in the way we live.

CHECKPOINT
Notice why the Lifestyle section changed.

CHECKPOINT
What purpose does this section serve?

wrap up

1. Watch the Lifestyle section in your local newspaper for one week. Make a list of the types of articles and features it includes. Share your findings in a small group.

2. The Lifestyle section is intended to reflect and address changes in the way we live. Write a short paragraph explaining how the Lifestyle section in your local newspaper does that. Include clippings to illustrate your points.

Bill advances to limit junk food in schools

warm up

Get out a piece of paper and jot down all the things you ate or are planning to eat today. Highlight or underline those items that are healthy and those that would be classified as junk food. Compare your list with a classmate.

AMBER McDOWELL, *THE ASSOCIATED PRESS*, APRIL 29, 2004

NASHVILLE — Legislation to limit the sale of junk food and soft drinks in Tennessee schools advanced in the General Assembly Wednesday.

Both the Senate and House education committees voted unanimously for the bill, which would authorize the state Board of Education to set nutrition standards for food sold in vending machines at schools with students in kindergarten through 8th grade. The new rules would be implemented for the 2005-2006 school year.

The bill now moves on for debate by the full membership of each chamber.

The bill's supporters want to replace sodas, candy bars, and potato chips currently sold in vending machines with more nutritious choices such as grain products, fruit and fruit juices, vegetables and vegetable juices, water, dairy products, sports drinks, and nuts and seeds.

CHECKPOINT
What types of food are sold in your school cafeteria?

43

"We're being inconsistent. We're trying to teach kids about what foods to eat for their health while they're in class, and then they walk out and the halls are lined with vending machines" full of unhealthy foods, said Rep. Joe Fowlkes, D-Cornersville, who sponsored the measure in the House.

According to the American Dietetic Association, children consuming soft drinks take in an average of 200 extra calories a day, which can translate to a weight gain of about 2 pounds per month.

CHECKPOINT

How does drinking soft drinks affect weight gain?

"Vending machines are great nutritional education tools in schools," said Nan Allison of the Tennessee Dietetic Association.

"From moment to moment, hour to hour, they are reinforcement for kids" on healthy eating.

Tennessee has the nation's third-highest rate of obesity and one of the highest rates of Type 2 diabetes among schoolchildren, according to a coalition of bill supporters that includes the Tennessee Medical Association, Tennessee Nurses Association, and Tennessee School Health Coalition. Type 2 diabetes is strongly linked to poor diet and being overweight.

The bill also would require the state Board of Education to set similar nutrition standards for individual or a la carte foods sold in school cafeterias, such as sports drinks.

The measure, which has been in development for about three years, was applauded by members of the Senate Education Committee.

"This is a national issue ... that is timely, that is relevant, that will make

a difference in the lives of a lot of people," said Sen. Roscoe Dixon, D-Memphis.

But committee member Sen. Bill Ketron warned his colleagues that the bill, sponsored by Sen. Larry Trail, D-Murfreesboro, was just a start. For children to truly lead healthier lives, he said, schools must motivate them to exercise by reinstating physical education programs cut in recent years because of tight budgets.

"Until we do that, we're only addressing one side of the future of our children," said Ketron, R-Murfreesboro.

wrap up

1. Conduct a survey among your classmates to determine their eating habits. Are the results in line with the findings in the article?

2. Work with the members of your class to develop a campaign to promote healthy eating. Make posters and advertisements with a slogan you have made up.

Why milk is at rear of the store

Consultants advise stores on how to sell. Service should be top priority, they say.

warm up

Before reading the article, try to answer the question in the headline. Why do you think milk is at the rear of the store?

CHECKPOINT
Who are Kizer & Bender and why might stores want to hire them?

STACI STURROCK, *THE PALM BEACH POST*, OCTOBER 27, 2004

West Palm Beach, FLA. — Why do supermarkets insist on stocking milk in the back corner? ...

As Kizer & Bender, the pair, headquartered in St. Charles, Ill., size up stores nationwide and help retailers serve shoppers better — they increase profit margins in the process.

"Customer service is the competitive battle-field," they once wrote in a craft-industry newsletter. "If you don't do it well, you lose. Period."

Among the things we learned after shopping with them: If you want to keep a lid on spending, browse alone.

"One woman shopping is good," Bender says, but from the retailer's perspective, "two or more women shopping is better. We egg each other on. ..."

They encourage you to explore the store.

"Most stores will put seasonal (merchandise) up front, to get you in the spirit right away," Bender says. They'll follow with year-round inventory, saving the most basic supplies for the back. That's why shoppers must navigate past tempting goodies to find milk in the farthest reaches of the grocery store.

CHECKPOINT

What is seasonal merchandise? What is an example?

They make you part of the extended family.

People want to shop at a place where they are known, or where they're at least part of "the club." Many retailers now reinforce their bond with customers by sending regular e-mails detailing sales and the arrival of new collections. ...

They tempt you to reach out and touch stuff.

Touch is incredibly important to shoppers,

so Kizer & Bender advise their employees to not continuously fold T-shirts, for example, in the middle of the store.

When shoppers see employees constantly straightening a display, they're reluctant to touch the items. "And people need to be able to touch things," Bender says.

They subtly tempt you to super-size it.

CHECKPOINT

What is meant by "super-sizing"?

When arranging two sizes of laundry detergent, smart store owners will put the larger jug on the right. Most people are right-handed, so they automatically reach for the item on that side.

They cross-merchandise.

They hang strips of scissors and tape near the gift wrap. They make sure tissue packets are near the cough syrup. They stock batteries next to toys that use them.

wrap up

1. Read carefully through the article again and make a list of all the suggestions it contains for retailers. Using your list of suggestions as a guide, create a diagram of how a grocery store might position its merchandise.

2. Using your list of suggestions, create an advertisement for the services of Kizer & Bender. Share your advertisement with some of your classmates.

ACKNOWLEDGMENTS

The publisher gratefully acknowledges the following for permission to reprint copyrighted material in this book.

Every reasonable effort has been made to trace the owners of copyrighted material and to make due acknowledgment. Any errors or omissions drawn to our attention will be gladly rectified in future editions.

Steve Barker: "Train dogs, parents and kids." *The Toronto Sun*, Letter of the Day. 27 October, 2004. Permission courtesy of *The Toronto Sun*.

Mike Bell: "Avril — Growing up in the spotlight's glare." *The Calgary Sun*, 1 April, 2004. Permission courtesy of *The Calgary Sun*.

Renée Graham: "Vintage U2 finds what it's looking for." *The Boston Globe*, 25 May 2005. This work is protected by copyright and the making of this copy was with the permission of *Access Copyright*. Any alteration of its content or futher copyright in any form whatsoever is strictly prohibited.

Robert Lee Hotz: "Humans' ancestral tree adds a twig." *Los Angeles Times*, 28 October 2004. Copyright, 2004, *Los Angeles Times*. Reprinted with permission.

Kelly Pedro: "Mom held, dad hit, daughters charged." *London Free Press*, 30 November 2004. Permission courtesy of *London Free Press*.

Staci Sturrock: "Why milk is at rear of the store." *The Palm Beach Post*, 27 October, 2004. Copyright 2004, *The Palm Beach Post*. Permission courtesy of *The Palm Beach Post*.

Nicolaas van Rijn: "Monster's Voyage of Destruction." Reprinted with permission — Torstar Syndication Services. From an article originally appearing in *The Toronto Star*, 27 December, 2004.

Brian Wong: "CD Reviews." Permission courtesy of Brian Wong.

"Bill advances to limit junk food in schools." ©Copyright. Associated Press. All rights reserved. Distributed by Valeo IP. Valeo Clearance License 3.5721.4687503-108421.

"Boy rescued four days after Japan quake." By Associated Press. *The Globe and Mail*, 27 October 2004. Permission courtesy of Valeo IP. Valeo Clearance License 3.5648.3360740-107419.

"Canadian juniors loaded with talent; NHL-calibre players included on big, skilful squad." By The Canadian Press. *Kitchener-Waterloo Record*, 17 December 2004. Permission courtesy of The Canada Press.

"Parental Guidance." *The Calgary Herald*, 31 May 1995. Reprinted with permission of *The Calgary Herald*.